P9-CIT-465

Mars

Quinn M. Arnold

CREATIVE EDUCATION
CREATIVE PAPERBACKS

seedlings

Published by Creative Education and Creative Paperbacks
P.O. Box 227, Mankato, Minnesota 56002
Creative Education and Creative Paperbacks
are imprints of The Creative Company
www.thecreativecompany.us

Design by Ellen Huber; production by Joe Kahnke
Art direction by Rita Marshall
Printed in the United States of America

Photographs by Alamy (Design Pics Inc.), Creative Commons
Wikimedia (NASA/JPL-Caltech/University of Arizona), Getty
Images (DEA/G. DAGLI ORTI, Detlev van Ravenswaay), NASA
(NASA/JPL-Caltech, NASA/JPL-CALTECH/MALIN SPACE
SCIENCES SYSTEMS, NASA/JPL-Caltech/MSSS), Science Source
(Ludek Pesek, Detlev van Ravenswaay), Shutterstock (Serhii
Kalaba, muratart, NASA images, PLRANG ART, Vadim Sadovski),
SuperStock (Stocktrek Images)

Library of Congress Cataloging-in-Publication Data
Names: Arnold, Quinn M., author.
Title: Mars / Quinn M. Arnold.
Series: Seedlings.
Includes bibliographical references and index.
Summary: A kindergarten-level introduction to the planet
Mars, covering its orbital process, its moons, and such
defining features as its rocks, dust storms, and name.
Identifiers: ISBN 978-1-60818-915-1 (hardcover) / ISBN 978-1-
62832-531-7 (pbk) / ISBN 978-1-56660-967-8 (eBook)
This title has been submitted for CIP
processing under LCCN 2017938979.

CCSS: RI.K.1, 2, 3, 4, 5, 6, 7;
RI.1.1, 2, 3, 4, 5, 6, 7; RF.K.1, 3; RF.1.1

First Edition HC 9 8 7 6 5 4 3 2 1
First Edition PBK 9 8 7 6 5 4 3 2 1

TABLE OF CONTENTS

Hello, Mars!

Mars is the fourth planet from the sun.

The "Red Planet" is rocky and icy. It is cold and cloudy there.

Dust storms blow across Mars.

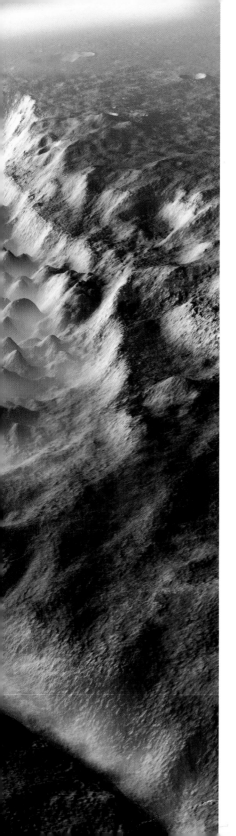

Sometimes the storms cover the small planet. They can last for months.

Two small moons
circle Mars.

They are called Phobos
and Deimos. *Phobos*
means "fear." *Deimos*
means "panic."

Mars takes almost two
years to circle the sun.
Mars has deep canyons.

It has the tallest volcano in our solar system.

Astronomers study planets.

They found Mars thousands of years ago. Mars is named for an old story about the god of war.

Space rocks
crash into Mars.

Winds blow dust
and clouds.

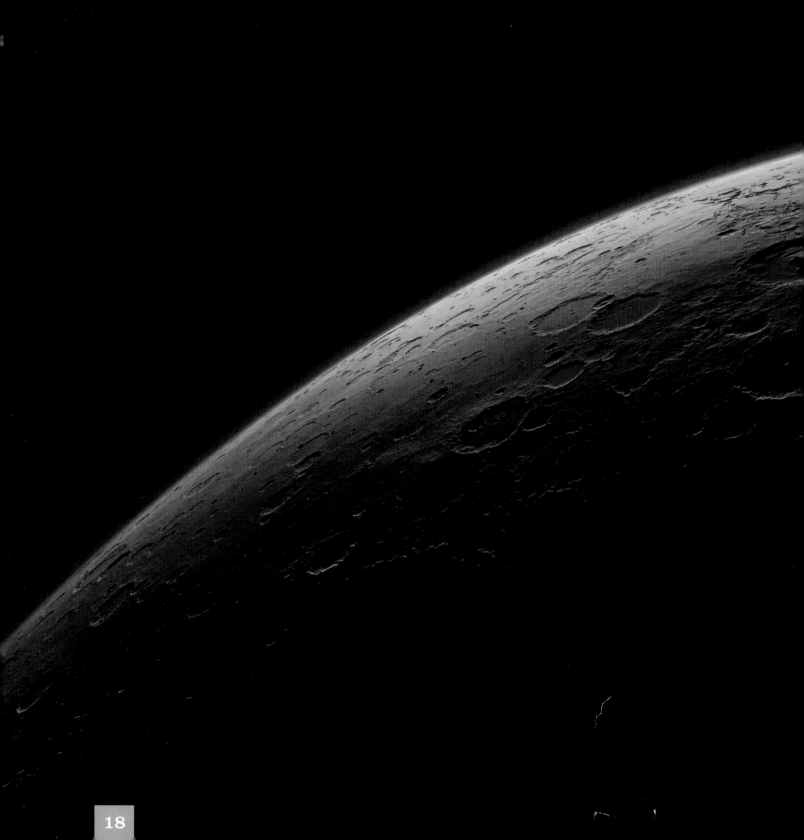

Goodbye, Mars!

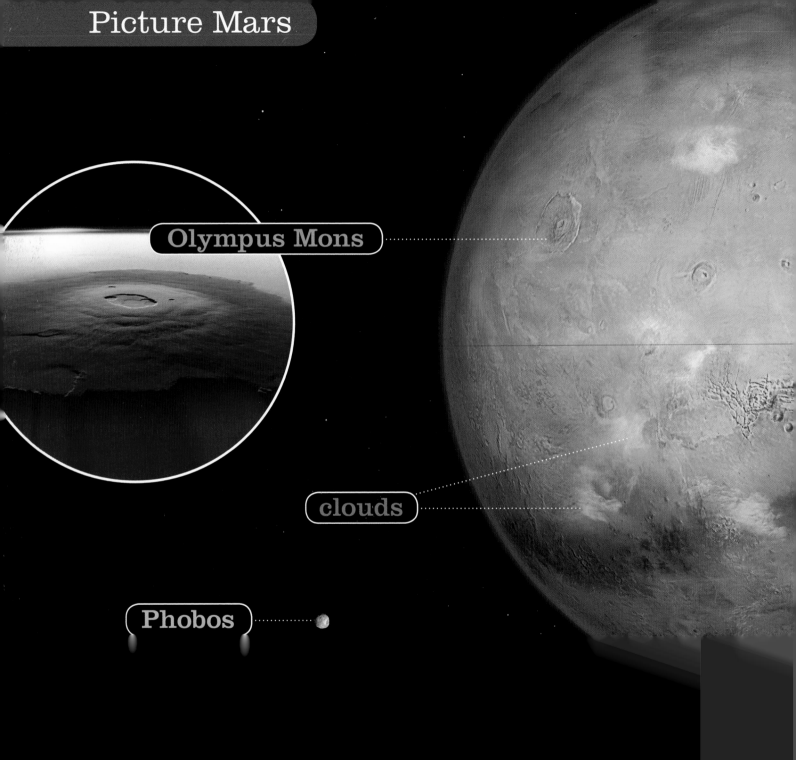

Picture Mars

Olympus Mons

clouds

Phobos

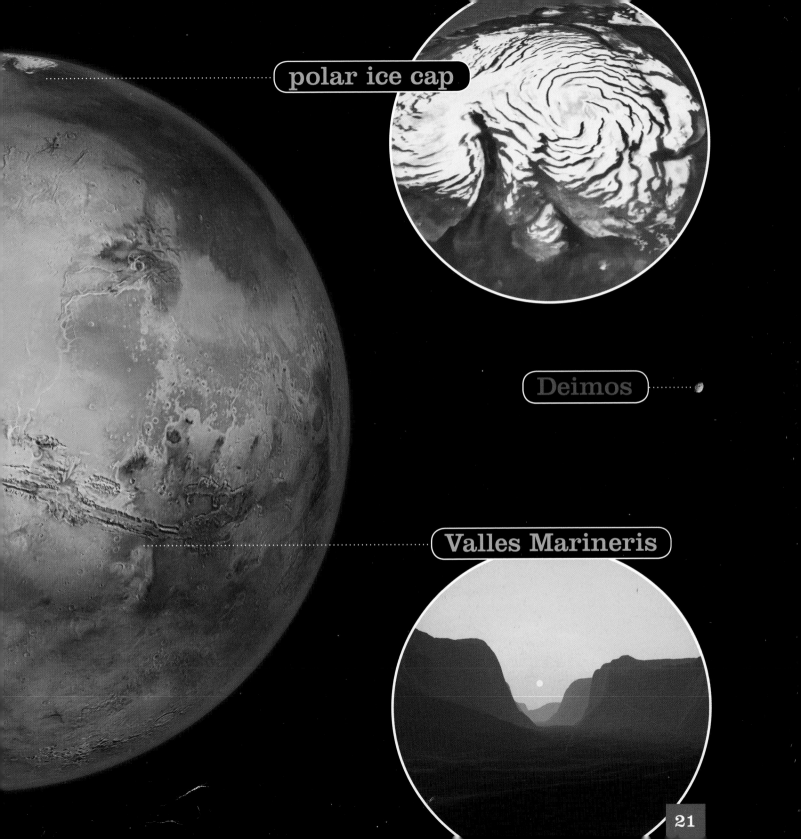

polar ice cap

Deimos

Valles Marineris

Words to Know

god: a being thought to have special powers and control over the world

planet: a rounded object that moves around a star

solar system: the sun, the planets, and their moons

volcano: a mountain with a hole on top that sometimes sends out rocks, ash, and lava

Read More

Adamson, Thomas K. *Do You Really Want to Visit Mars?*
Mankato, Minn.: Amicus, 2014.

Loewen, Nancy. *Seeing Red: The Planet Mars.*
Minneapolis: Picture Window Books, 2008.

Websites

NASA: Mars for Kids
http://mars.jpl.nasa.gov/participate/funzone/
Build your own Mars spacecraft or play a game.

National Geographic Kids: Mission to Mars
http://kids.nationalgeographic.com/explore/space/mission
-to-mars/#mars-planet.jpg
Learn how Mars moves through the solar system.

Index

Phobos